*Remembering*
# Florida Tourist Attractions

**Steve Rajtar**

TURNER
PUBLISHING COMPANY

Henry Plant built the Tampa Bay Hotel to attract railroad passengers. It opened in 1891 at a cost of $3 million, featuring a Moorish Revival style modeled after the Alhambra Palace in Granada, Spain. There are 12 towers with bulbous domes and cupolas, ornate porches, and covered cornices. The former resort now houses the University of Tampa.

*Remembering*
# Florida Tourist Attractions

Turner Publishing Company
4507 Charlotte Avenue • Suite 100
Nashville, Tennessee 37209
(615) 255-2665

*Remembering Florida Tourist Attractions*

www.turnerpublishing.com

Library of Congress Control Number: 2010924324

ISBN: 978-1-59652-667-9

ISBN: 978-1-68336-829-8 (pbk)

Printed in the United States of America

# CONTENTS

# Acknowledgments

This volume, *Remembering Florida Tourist Attractions,* is the result of the cooperation and efforts of many individuals and organizations. It is with great thanks that we acknowledge the valuable contribution of the Library of Congress, the State Archives of Florida, and the many photographers and collectors who have shared their images of the state by donating them to the Florida Photographic Collection.

We would also like to thank the hundreds of millions of tourists who have visited Florida since the state was new, eager to pay for the opportunity to be entertained and amazed. Without their curiosity, most of the attractions depicted in this book would not have existed.

In 1955, the Gulfarium opened in Fort Walton Beach with a porpoise theme. Porpoises performed in the large pool. Porpoises were shown on posters and signs throughout the park. The sign along the road showed a porpoise outlined in neon, constantly jumping through a hoop. The attraction is still entertaining porpoise fans today.

# INTRODUCTION

Since the earliest days following its discovery by Europeans in the 1500s, Florida has been attracting visitors who seek adventure, wealth, escape from civilization, and opportunities to set up their own businesses to attract the dollars of others. Early tourist attractions were comparatively simple, some consisting merely of natural phenomena such as spouting artesian wells, clear spring waters, large or unusual trees, or a variety of ways to view and enjoy the flora, fauna, water, and sunshine.

Many of the early attractions were little more than small exhibits of curious objects or animals. A structure of coral or a collection of parts of trees might bring in visitors willing to pay a nominal amount, just enough to keep the attraction in existence.

The late 1800s also ushered in an era of elaborate hotels, themselves intended to be tourist destinations. Resorts with golf courses, water sports, and gourmet food became popular, especially with wealthy Northern industrialists riding the new railroads.

Things changed drastically in Florida on October 1, 1971. That day, the huge, modern Walt Disney World opened near Orlando with special effects to entertain and amaze, and bring back visitors again and again. The opening of Walt Disney World constituted a challenge to all other tourist attractions to grow and impress and modernize. Some did and today still exist, but many could not compete and soon went out of business. A few retain their mom-and-pop character and enjoy some success in diverting tourists drawn to the mega-parks, which advertise everywhere.

To a significant number of travelers around the world, Florida tourism means Orlando and nearby areas. In addition to Walt Disney World, consisting not only of the Magic Kingdom but also of MGM Studios, water parks, Animal Kingdom, EPCOT, Pleasure Island, and other attractions, there are Sea World, Universal Studios, and several other parks designed to draw in tourist dollars. Nearby US 192 heading into Kissimmee is essentially a strip of tourist attractions.

Before 1971, however, Central Florida was not as important as a tourist destination. Vacationers traveling to Florida generally headed for the beaches. They went there for the sand, surf, and sun, but also for the man-made attractions. Panama City, St. Augustine, Miami, Sarasota, and other cities close to the water were where these tourist attractions sprang up. The central part of the state, with its clear springs and geological formations, attracted many who wanted to swim and spend the day with nature, but the coasts were where unusual entertainment could be found.

Early Florida was full of animals not to be found in other parts of the country, other than in zoos. Entrepreneurs found ways to display them and charge admission fees. Performing porpoises were popular at Ocean World, Theater of the Sea, Gulfarium, Aquatarium, and Marineland. Colorful birds populated Jungle Land, McKee Jungle Gardens, the Miami Rare Bird Farm, Sunken Gardens, and the Everglades Wonder Gardens. Snakes were featured at Rattlesnake, Ross Allen's Reptile Institute, the Miami Serpentarium, and Sarasota Reptile Farm and Zoo. Of course, alligators attracted the curious to the St. Augustine Alligator Farm, and to Casper's Ostrich and Alligator Farm, which, along with the Florida Ostrich Farm in Jacksonville, had tourists getting up close and personal with a bird definitely not from Florida.

Some of the popular attractions were and still are the homes of famous individuals, including Marjorie Kinnan Rawlings, Thomas Edison, and Ernest Hemingway. Other homes are visited because they are impressive to look at, such as the Gamble Mansion or the Gregory home in Torreya State Park. Native Americans were living displays at Musa Isle Indian Village.

Traditional amusement-park rides attracted adventure seekers to Daytona Beach and Panama City Beach, as well as Dixieland Park in Jacksonville. Many attractions included train rides, some of which ran on tracks and others which were trams disguised as trains.

Florida's multifaceted history was evident in its many museums. Historical events were recalled at the John Gorrie State Museum (the invention of air conditioning), the Constitution Convention Museum (Florida's becoming a state), Spanish Village (the settlement of the state by Spaniards), and the House of Refuge Museum at Gilbert's Bar (shipwrecks and rescues), to name a few. Some of the early events were also memorialized in plays which attracted thousands over the years, including Cross and Sword and the Black Hills Passion Play.

Other museums displayed just about anything one could think of, including clocks (St. Cloud China and Clock Museum), collections of just about everything (St. Augustine's Lightner Museum), religious carvings (Prince of Peace Memorial), and a petrified cat (the T. T. Wentworth, Jr. Museum). One of the most unusual was the Cypress Knee Museum, where a piece of polished wood could be purchased that resembled any person or thing imaginable—provided one had a good imagination.

If someone thought tourists would pay to visit a garden, or a thrill ride, or a show, such a facility was likely to be created and publicized. Often, visitors driving the back roads of Florida would come upon the attractions and spend their time and money viewing whatever was there. They would likely purchase souvenirs of the day to take back home and entice others to visit Florida and see the sites for themselves.

The demise of many of these small attractions can be attributed to two leading causes. First, traffic was reduced when the Florida Turnpike and other main highways routed tourists away from the back roads. No longer was a family from the north likely to happen upon what appeared to be an interesting sign or building, and decide to park and visit. Second, the opening of Walt Disney World and the other very large parks gave tourists specific destinations. They weren't headed to Florida anymore to see what they could find. Instead, they headed to the highly publicized parks, missing everything that couldn't be seen from the airports or interstate highways.

Driving through Florida today, one sees only the large theme parks and their billboards. Fifty or a hundred years ago, the scene was much different, and what attracted tourist dollars then would be ignored by most tourists now. On the pages that follow are images of some of Florida's attractions of yesteryear—those in existence before the opening of Walt Disney World. Come reminisce about times when it took less to amuse, less to amaze, and far fewer dollars to pay for it all.

This home was built between 1880 and 1900 as a four-room cottage with a narrow, open front porch and a back wing containing a dining room and kitchen. Author Marjorie Kinnan Rawlings bought it in 1928 and enlarged it. She divided her time between a home in St. Augustine and this one in Cross Creek, where she wrote most of her books, including *The Yearling, Cross Creek, Jacob's Ladder, South Moon Under, Golden Apples, The Secret River, When the Whippoorwill,* and *The Sojourner.* The Marjorie Kinnan Rawlings House was added to the National Register in 1970 and, as a state historic site, is open to the public.

The Miracle Strip Amusement Park was opened by Billy Lark in 1963 in Panama City Beach. The main attraction was the Starliner wooden roller coaster, and over the years it kept expanding with additional rides, including the Looper loop-o-plane, the Sea Dragon swinging boat, the Shockwave, a wave swinger, the Haunted Castle shown here, the Dungeon tilt-a-whirl, bumper cars, spinning teacups, and the Big Eli Ferris Wheel. Attendance dropped after 2001, and Labor Day 2004 was the park's last day of operation. It was estimated that more than 20 million had visited the park during its 41 years.

In the early 1960s, Panama City Beach's Ghost Town opened as a town of empty buildings, and the only live people were the tourists who came by to peek into their windows at fiberglass statues. Owned by the Churchwell family, after a few years and suggestions by the Lewis family, the old-looking buildings became occupied by shops where tourists could spend money on food and souvenirs. Staged street shoot-outs between a marshal and a bad guy began in 1966. J. E. Churchwell shortly thereafter combined the western-themed area with a roller coaster and other amusement-park rides to form another tourist attraction, Petticoat Junction.

Jungle Land was a jungle-themed park built in Panama City Beach in 1966. It featured a waterfall and live alligators, an artificial volcano that spewed smoke, and pathways that took tourists along the "Journey to the Center of the Earth" with its blacklight lava pits and skeletal remains. During the late 1970s, the attraction closed, and in 1981 the property was acquired by Alvin's Island Tropical Department Store and renamed Alvin's Magic Mountain Mall. Today, some of the original construction is present, along with live alligators and other animals. Shown here is the park's appearance in 1969-70, before it became a retail store selling swimsuits and other tropical items.

A young girl poses with four parrots at Jungle Land, Panama City Beach.

Lee Koplin built several miniature golf courses across the country in 1948-58 and coined the name Goofy Golf for a course in Mississippi. In 1959, he built a Goofy Golf course in Panama City Beach, including a rocket ship, monkey, octopus, sphinx, windmill, mechanized alligator, castle, brontosaurus, and wooden ship, which constituted obstacles for the putters and unusual sites to attract attention from the highway and while waiting for other golfers to play. They were eerily illuminated for play at night. In the middle of the golf course next to the brontosaurus, Koplin built his family's home. The original Panama City Beach Goofy Golf was just the first of many oddball courses in the area.

A dragon munches on sightseers at Lee Koplin's Goofy Golf.

Panama City Beach's Petticoat Junction was popular in the 1960s with a carousel, train ride, and typical amusement-park attractions. Its wooden Tornado roller coaster was designed by John Allen of the Philadelphia Toboggan Company and was built in 1962 at Wedgewood Village Amusement Park in Oklahoma City. A portion of it was moved in 1968 to Petticoat Junction, where the ride was redesigned and rebuilt. The park closed in 1984 and most of the rides and attractions were auctioned off the following year. The train station was abandoned and became part of an RV park. Much of the land where the rides once thrilled visitors became the home of a Wal-Mart.

In 1932, Gid Thomas began development of 104 acres as Panama City Beach with a 12-room hotel. It opened in 1936 and soon after was acquired by J. E. Churchwell, who built tourist cottages as part of his Long Beach Resort. The original attraction was the white-sand beach, as shown in this photo from the mid-1950s. The Churchwell family included conveniences like restaurants, a skating rink, and an amusement park, which, by the late 1960s, had overwhelmed the original beach theme. On August 12, 1970, Long Beach merged with West Panama City Beach, Edgewater Gulf Beach, and Panama City Beach to become a single tourist mecca, Panama City Beach.

Soon after the creation of NASA in 1958, its facility at Cape Canaveral (named Kennedy Space Center in 1963) set up outdoor displays and began bus tours, which have evolved into one of Florida's most popular tourist attractions. Shown here are visitors viewing early rockets on display in 1961.

Pirates World opened in Dania in 1966. It had a pirate theme, superposed onto exciting old-fashioned thrill rides. The Crows Nest observation tower had been known as the Belgian Aerial Tower when it stood at the 1964 New York World's Fair, the same place the log flume ride began. The 1897 steeplechase ride came from Coney Island. Other popular items were a Wild Mouse roller coaster, spiral slides, a paratrooper, ski-ball, and other midway games. Rock concerts were also held there. Attendance dropped off after the opening of Walt Disney World, and the park went bankrupt in 1973. It closed for good in 1975 and condominiums were later built on the site.

In 1926, the Dania Indian Reservation was added to the Seminole Nation of Florida, then was renamed the Hollywood Indian Reservation in 1966. Depicted here is the small Seminole Museum located at the reservation in Dania in 1958.

Pioneer City opened in Dania in 1966 and featured the typical western town, shoot-outs, stagecoach rides, and saloon shows available in other parks in Osprey, Silver Springs, Panama City, and Brooksville. It had trouble attracting tourists and disappeared within a few years. The land was redeveloped as the StoneBrook Estates community.

Ocean World in Ft. Lauderdale featured popular dolphin shows, as well as alligators, sea lions, and sharks. In 1978, Dr. David Nathanson began doing "dolphin human therapy" language research there, using dolphins to teach children with Down Syndrome. Ocean World closed in 1994 and the animals were moved to similar tourist attractions.

Ft. Lauderdale's International Swimming Hall of Fame opened in 1965 with an induction which included Olympic swimmer and movie star Johnny Weissmuller. More than 40 exhibits trace the history of the aquatic sports of swimming, diving, water polo, and synchronized swimming. Displays include Olympic artifacts, uniforms, and medals.

After decades as a quiet park, Homosassa Springs became a popular tourist attraction in the 1960s. In addition to the floating observatory—which allowed the viewing of fish—and trails that wound through the woods, the park featured the Ivan Tors celebrity animals from TV and movies. The Citrus County site is now a state park emphasizing its wildlife.

Located at a bend of the St. Johns River, Green Cove Springs was believed to have great healing powers. The springs drew many who were suffering a variety of maladies. According to legend, pirates visited the site in the early days to fill their casks with the sulfur water.

Dr. Henry Nehrling, whose collection of tropical plants had been damaged by a freeze in Orange County in 1917, acquired land in Naples in 1919, where he expected a warmer clime. After his death in 1929, the gardens were largely ignored until the 1950s, when Julius Fleischmann cleared a trail, cleaned out debris, and added tropical birds to the area, which he named Caribbean Gardens. During 1967, Larry and Jane Tetzlaff became interested in the park and reopened it in 1969 with many species of tropical animals. The park, now known as the Naples Zoo, has become a breeding center for several species, and visitors flock to take the Primate Expedition Cruise and stroll past the varied habitats.

Jacksonville's Dixieland Park opened on March 9, 1907, south of the St. Johns River. Along a pedestrian mall were typical rides, including a 160-foot roller coaster and the "Flying Jenny," a carrousel with 56 wooden animals. There were real animals, too—camels, elephants, horses, and tigers—when the park was used for filming movies with a jungle theme. Buildings included a palace of industry and a large cafe and dance pavilion. It was a venue for concerts and sports, including ostrich racing and baseball games. The great Babe Ruth once played in a game there. After World War I, its popularity faded, and little is left except for Treaty Oak, an ancient tree with a 160-foot-wide crown.

In 1941, the Jacksonville Children's Museum was created and in 1948 it moved into the Victorian house shown here. The museum moved into a modern building in 1969, then shifted its focus from the hands-on exhibits just for children to an orientation for adults and children. It was renamed the Museum of Arts & Science in 1977, and since 1988 has been the Museum of Science & History.

In 1907, a municipal park opened near downtown Jacksonville and was named Dignan Park for the chairman of the Board of Public Works. In the park was the city's first supervised playground. The park received national attention when it was selected for the 1914 annual reunion of the United Confederate Veterans, and because of the event the name was changed to Confederate Park. In 1915, the Woman of the South monument was unveiled to honor the contributions of women to the Confederacy. Another popular feature of Confederate Park is the Rose Arbor, shown here in 1934.

Jacksonville's Florida Ostrich Farm was a popular place to visit beginning in 1888 and continued at least into the 1940s. The facility featured ostrich races including trotters such as Oliver W., who pulled carts carrying jockeys around an oval track. The Florida farm had its summer home during the first two decades of the twentieth century in Saratoga County, New York. In addition to racing, the more than 200 ostriches kept at the Florida farm produced feathers costing up to $40 each, used for high-fashion ladies' hats. Breeding pairs were kept in corrals and younger birds were allowed to wander in large enclosures, with warnings to tourists about how dangerous they could be.

To celebrate the 400th anniversary of the founding of Pensacola in 1959, a replica of a 1723 Spanish village was constructed on Pensacola Beach. It was the center of attention for the quadricentennial celebration, and continued to attract tourists to see its varied structures. The exteriors lacked ornamentation, but the interiors were decorated with period furniture and accessories, and they were occupied by reenactors in costume, doing what eighteenth-century Spaniards did in Pensacola. In 1973, the structures had deteriorated beyond the point where they could accommodate tourists, and were razed.

Along Pensacola's East Government Street is the Seville Quarter, which includes eight saloons and restaurants. Bob Snow, a trumpet player and Dixieland band leader who had done flight training in Pensacola, came back to the city to develop this entertainment complex, which opened in 1967. His partner, Wilmer Mitchell, is now the owner of the popular place to eat and socialize, with Rosie O'Gradey's Good Time Emporium, Apple Annie's, Lili Marlene's World War I Aviators Pub, the Palace Oyster Bar, Fast Eddie's Billiard Parlor, Phineas Phogg's Balloon Works, Heritage Hall, and End O' the Alley Bar. The complex was the model for a similar development by Snow in Orlando in the 1970s.

The second-largest aviation museum in the country is the National Museum of Naval Aviation, located at the Pensacola Naval Air Station. It grew out of a need to expose naval flight trainees to the history of naval aviation, and a desire to improve public relations with civilians. Military personnel raised funds in the Pensacola area, resulting in the opening of the museum in 1963, with eight aircraft displayed in a World War II vintage building. In 1975, a new structure increased the display space from 8,500 to 68,000 square feet. Expansions in 1980 and 1990 increased that to 250,000 square feet. The Emil Buehler Naval Aviation Library opened as part of the complex in 1992.

The John Gorrie State Museum honors the doctor who devised an experimental machine to cool the rooms of malaria patients. It had a problem in that its pipes would clog with ice, but he was able to work with that to produce an ice-making machine. That in turn evolved into air conditioning. Gorrie received the first United States patent for mechanical refrigeration in 1851, but his venture to manufacture the machine failed. Humiliated by critics, impoverished, and his health broken, he died in 1855 and is buried in Gorrie Square in Apalachicola. A replica of his machine is shown here on display at the museum, which opened in November 1957. Located in Apalachicola, it also features displays on local history, fishing, cotton, and the lumber industry.

In the 1930s, Tom Gaskins began collecting cypress knees, the knobby wooden protuberances at the base of cypress trees. He found that many resembled people, animals, or familiar objects. Gaskins opened his Cypress Knee Museum along US 27 in Palmdale, displaying his collection (along with labels stating what he thought the knees resembled) and selling polished specimens to customers.

Tom Gaskins is shown here with one of his showpiece cypress knees. The tourist flow dropped off with the opening of the Florida Turnpike and interstates 75 and 95. Gaskins died in 1998, the Lykes Company mandated the removal of Gaskins' famous signs from several tracts of pasture along main roads, and thieves stole the best pieces in 2000, resulting in the museum's closing.

The first proposed constitution of Florida was signed on January 11, 1839, at the constitutional convention held at St. Joseph, a small town destroyed in 1841 by a tidal wave and yellow fever epidemic. It was rebuilt as Port St. Joe, and in that city the convention monument shown here was constructed in 1922. The city donated it to the state in 1950, followed in 1954 by a donation of adjacent land. On the 13.5 acres in 1955, the state opened the Constitution Convention Museum so that visitors could relive the events which took Florida from a territory into statehood. Included is a replica of the west wing of the original Convention Hall.

Weeki Wachee Springs, developed in 1946-47 by swimming star Newton Perry, is known for its mermaids and other underwater performers, such as Marian Tolar, shown here in 1949. The park at the Hernando County spring, which produces 170 million gallons of water daily, offers much more, including an animal show, swimming area, and a riverboat ride. In 1959, Weeki Wachee's popularity increased when it was purchased by the American Broadcasting Company, which promoted it and built a 500-seat underwater theater. It remains popular with tourists.

In 1900, Dr. J. H. Mills purchased Sulphur Springs and land north of the Hillsborough River, which had been used for decades by those seeking the springs' healing powers. He added a dance pavilion, swimming pool, and Ferris wheel. Later additions included a toboggan slide, gazebo, alligator farm, and arcade, some of which appear in this 1920 image. The Sulphur Springs Hotel and Arcade was built in 1926 with a double-tiered arcade along the front, which sheltered the sidewalk. It was torn down in 1967. In 1927, a 210-foot-tall water tower was added. In 2002, the area was purchased by the city of Tampa and turned into the public River Tower Park.

Tampa's initial electric trolley line began in 1892 and linked downtown, Ballast Point, Ybor City, and West Tampa. Later, while it was controlled by Emelia Chapin, three acres were purchased at the Ballast Point end of the trolley line (shown here) to be transformed into a park, first called Jules Verne Park. The early park was used as a pleasure resort for tourists and locals, and was renamed Ballast Point Park because ships dumped their ballast there.

Rattlesnake was a 1930s village that grew up around George K. End's general store and snake pit attraction. In addition to selling rattlesnake meat, he sold venom to treat snakebites but died of a bite from one of his own rattlers. In the 1950s, the area was annexed into Tampa.

Now known as the county's Fred Ball Park, this began as the Palma Ceia Spring, a popular swimming spot from the early days. A fountain there is engraved with the date "1906." A large Venetian swimming pool was constructed behind the spring around 1928, but was eliminated when the flow from the spring became insufficient to keep it filled. During the 1980s, the Tampa Garden Club spent more than $12,000 to improve the surrounding grounds, including the erection of a gazebo. Today's park is named for a local government official, who in 1942 headed a movement to have Hillsborough County purchase the spring.

Tampa's Lowry Park became the home of the area's first zoo when it outgrew Plant Park and acquired larger animals, such as the elephant donated by Sumter Lowry in 1961. That donation motivated the city to expand the zoo and add rides, shows, and the Fairyland Village children's storybook park, reached by the Rainbow Bridge shown here.

Arthur McKee hired William Lyman Phillips to set out a wilderness park along US 1 in Vero Beach. What resulted was McKee Jungle Gardens, which opened to the public in 1932. The initial focus was on the trees and other plants, but after World War II attention shifted to tropical animals. The park also featured giant concrete mushrooms and young women dressed in outfits similar to those worn in Tarzan movies. A reduced number of visitors forced the park to close in 1976, and 62 of the original 80 acres became the site of condominiums. The remaining land was acquired in 1995 by a group who restored the area and reopened it as McKee Botanical Garden in 2001.

The tiny town of Two Egg has never had a museum or zoo or anything unusual (unless one counts Lloyd Earl McMullian's antique engine collection, shown here), yet tourists stop there. Some come to steal the town's sign, the most frequently taken one in Florida. Others come to the Lawrence Grocery, the town's only store, to purchase T-shirts and baseball caps with the name of the town and to ask where the name "Two Egg" came from. There are many theories, but the generally accepted one involves the children of Will Williams, who were in the store trading two home-grown eggs for candy. When a traveling salesman noticed this, he called the place Two Egg and the name stuck.

Florida Caverns State Park in Marianna came into being in 1935 as part of the state's push to employ those who were needy as a result of the Great Depression. While the Works Progress Administration and Civilian Conservation Corps funneled tax dollars into building park facilities during 1937, a surveyor noticed a hole near a fallen tree. He crawled in and found what is now known as the Florida Caverns Tour Cave. A crew worked on the two-acre cave until 1942, when it was opened to the public. Today, rangers guide tourists along a route which passes stalactites and stalagmites, soda straw formations, stone draperies, and flowstones. The tour begins about 60 feet beneath the surface of the ground.

Just south of downtown Leesburg on the shore of Lake Harris are the beautiful 100-acre Venetian Gardens, which began as a project of the WPA in the mid-1930s, when this picture was taken. The canals and gardens have been a popular destination for those seeking a quiet place to spend some time among seven beautifully landscaped islands.

In 1936, brothers Bill and Lester Piper opened their wildlife exhibit in Bonita Springs along the Tamiami Trail. It began as the Bonita Springs Reptile Gardens, then attracted more tourists when the name was changed to the Everglades Wonder Gardens after World War II. The wildlife on display included black bears, flamingos, otters, snakes, panthers, alligators, and crocodiles. Bill Piper and an assistant are shown here capturing a treed bobcat in 1950. The park is now owned by Lester's grandson, David Piper, Jr.

In 1923, Alfred Barmore Maclay of New York purchased land near Lake Hall in Tallahassee and set out to construct his winter home and beautiful gardens. It was his goal to use both exotic and native plants to create scenic beauty—meant to soothe the senses and provide a place of peace. He called the project Killearn Gardens and used trees and shrubs as well as flowers, so that the property would provide an interesting visual effect year-round. In 1953, the Maclay family donated the home and gardens to the state, which renamed it Alfred B. Maclay Gardens State Park. The 307-acre park still provides a quiet place to get away from the hustle and bustle of the city.

In 1957, the Tallahassee Junior Museum was established to introduce children and others to nature, history, and cultures. Over the years, the focus has shifted to an emphasis on the Big Bend region's natural and cultural history since the nineteenth century. The first displays were placed in a house downtown. Today the museum (renamed the Tallahassee Museum of History and Natural Science) covers 52 acres and includes an 1880s farmstead, historic buildings including the Princess Catherine Murat house, nature trails through an area displaying native wildlife, the Discovery Center, and natural science exhibits.

Located near Chiefland is Manatee Springs State Park. In addition to camping, hiking, and boating, the 2,075-acre park features a large spring, which produces 117 million gallons of crystal clear water each day. The water flows down the spring to the Suwannee River and then to the Gulf of Mexico. The park was opened in 1955, and since then it has been a popular place for scuba divers and tourists alike. Divers can enjoy the open water or explore the underwater caves and caverns. Sightseers use the long boardwalk along the spring to watch for manatees, which give the area its name. The large aquatic mammals enjoy the 72-degree water year-round, especially from January through April.

This is the pre–Civil War home of Jason Gregory, moved during the 1930s to Torreya State Park on the east bank of the Apalachicola River. It is popular as a place for tours. The park is named after the rare torreya tree, which is found only near Bristol. Legend says the torreya is the "gopher wood" Noah used to build the Ark.

Minister Elvy Callaway concluded that since the Bristol area was the only place where gopher wood grew, and the Apalachicola was the world's only four-headed river system, it matched the Bible's description of the Garden of Eden. In the 1950s, Callaway and his followers erected signs and a gateway into a large natural ravine, which until Callaway's passing lured those who came to see whether Adam and Eve may have lived in Florida.

Silver Springs near Ocala began attracting tourists in 1860, when James Burt carried visitors to the area on steamboats to view the springs. In 1878, Hullam Jones installed a glass viewing box in the bottom of a canoe, which evolved into the famous glass-bottom boats, which switched from oar power to gasoline power in 1925. In the twentieth century, W. C. Ray and Shorty Davidson began promoting the park as a destination for those arriving by car. Additional features were added to augment the beautiful springs, including the Jungle Cruise with an island of monkeys, many of which swam away and whose descendants still populate the woods along the Silver River.

Six Gun Territory opened near Silver Springs in 1963 as the $2 million project of R. B. Coburn, who had just completed the construction of Ghost Town in the Sky in Maggie Valley, North Carolina. Six Gun Territory featured the typical old-looking western town and also had well-known actors signing autographs. The park closed in 1984.

This is an eight-spring carriage displayed at Silver Springs' Carriage Cavalcade in 1954. One of the early vehicle museums, it inspired Luray Caverns' Car and Carriage Caravan Cavalcade, which opened in Virginia later that same decade. Tourists could wander or ride aboard the Toonerville Trolley until the park closed in the early 1960s.

Ross Allen's Reptile Institute opened in 1929 at Silver Springs. Pictured here in the 1950s, Allen fascinated visitors by handling snakes and alligators. Focus later turned from entertainment to research, and until the 1970s the institute raised reptiles for zoos and collected venom to treat snakebites. Allen also featured an Indian village, populated by Seminoles.

Around 1963, the Early American Museum opened at the entrance to Silver Springs. Intended to recall the "good old days," displays included 101 vehicles, a 1910 fashion shop, 300 antique dolls, and a miniature animated model of an early circus. To represent recent American history, the museum included a full-scale model of a space capsule.

In the 1930s, the large spring near Dunnellon was renamed from Blue Springs to Rainbow Springs and "submarine boats" were brought in to show passengers the fish and springs through side windows below the waterline. The park is shown here in 1951.

Rainbow Springs could not attract the numbers that flocked to better-known springs around the state, but continued to exist as a smaller park with "mermaids" such as the one shown here in 1950. In 1967, the land was purchased by Walter Beinke who intended to make it a main destination with the addition of an aviary, rodeo, and monorail, but it lasted only until 1973. The site became a state park in 1990.

In Stuart, the displays in the Elliott Museum remind us what life was like during the nineteenth and twentieth centuries. Included are baseball memorabilia, antique automobiles, vintage clothing, life-size dioramas, and early inventions. Some of the displays are arranged as vintage stores, selling period shoes, drugs, and other items. The museum was founded in 1961 by Harmon Elliott to honor his father, Sterling. The Elliotts were inventors, and obtained 222 patents, many of which came from inventions on display in the museum, including Sterling's quadricycle. The museum operated by the Historical Society of Martin County also features workshops, educational programs, and children's art camps.

The building housing the House of Refuge Museum at Gilbert's Bar was constructed in 1876 as a life-saving station for victims of shipwrecks along the Florida coast near present-day Stuart. It was one of ten such stations commissioned by the U.S. Treasury Department, was manned by crews of the U.S. Lifesaving Service, and is the only such station remaining in Florida. The Historical Society of Martin County rescued it from deterioration in 1955 and turned it into a popular museum of four millennia of the history of Hutchinson Island, where it rests on a ridge overlooking both the Atlantic Ocean and the Indian River.

Ed Leedskalnin, who stood about 5 feet tall and weighed 100 pounds, constructed a rock garden at 28655 S. Dixie Highway in Homestead from 1,100 tons of coral boulders. His Coral Castle took him 28 years to build, and he claimed he did all the work himself, using homemade tools assembled from junk parts and the secrets used to build the ancient pyramids. The coral came from property Leedskalnin owned in Homestead and Florida City, two cities where he provided guided tours to raise money. He worked on the project from 1923 until he died in 1951, offering 10-cent tours to tourists who happened by. The Coral Castle is available for tours and for rental for birthdays, weddings, and other events.

Planned from the early 1940s by Fred D. Coppock and Captain W. B. Gray, the Miami Seaquarium opened to the public in 1955. Their intent was to build a large marine park, rather than a traditional aquarium. At the Seaquarium at 4400 Rickenbacker Causeway near Biscayne Bay, visitors can view ocean creatures through windows, ride through gardens on a monorail, or watch dolphins perform in a large pool. The park also treats injured marine mammals for release back into the ocean, and is a world leader in research on the endangered manatee.

Dolphins perform for tourists at the Miami Seaquarium in 1955.

From 1919 until 1964, the Musa Isle Indian Village along the Miami River attracted tourists who wanted to learn more about the Seminoles of Florida. They arrived on the double-decker *Seminole Queen,* which stopped at the village three times each day on its Miami River Island Cruise. Souvenirs could be purchased at the village's trading post at NW 25th Avenue at 16th Street, or visitors could watch natives supposedly in their natural habitat doing everyday things. These three Seminole medicine men pose for the camera in the 1910s.

Beginning in 1891, David Fairchild began a 37-year quest to collect plants from all over the world that could be used in the United States. In 1935, he moved to Miami and shared what he had learned with Colonel Robert H. Montgomery, who developed a botanical garden and named it the Fairchild Tropical Botanic Garden for his friend. Plant collector Montgomery opened the attraction in 1938 on 83 acres south of Miami, using the design of landscape architect William Lyman Phillips. Since then, additions have included the Rare Plant House, a library, the Hawkes Laboratory, and the Moos Sunken Garden. The garden is an active member of the American Association of Botanical Gardens.

Reptile expert William Haast ran his Miami Serpentarium in Pinecrest from 1948 to 1985, largely to focus attention on the previously unknown benefits of the use of snake venom in medical research. His handling of rattlesnakes, cobras, kraits, corals, bushmasters, mambas, and other deadly species—shown on the page opposite—attracted thousands of tourists, who sometimes witnessed him being bitten. Today, the business continues at an 88-acre facility in Punta Gorda as the Miami Serpentarium Laboratories, with an increased focus on research rather than entertainment. In 2003 at the age of 93, Haast suffered his 173rd poisonous bite and no longer personally milks his more than 400 poisonous snakes. He leaves that to younger workers.

This 1920s attraction was the Miami Beach Aquarium, also known as the Allison Aquarium, located at Fifth Street and the bay. In addition to attracting tourists, it also emphasized education. It had closed by 1928, whereupon the city moved some of its tanks to the *Prins Valdemar,* a former ship permanently moored as a tourist attraction.

James Deering, a co-founder of the International Harvester Company, hired hundreds of European craftsmen to build a winter retreat with an Italian Renaissance style along the shore of Miami's Biscayne Bay. What resulted in 1916 was Vizcaya, a 34-room villa to house the collection of antiques and art Deering accumulated during his world travels. The home has rooms furnished with styles including Renaissance, baroque, rococo, and neoclassical. Outside are formally landscaped gardens with fountains, statues, pools, and grottos. Tourists visit the mansion, shown here in a photograph taken from offshore around 1920, to tour the home, marvel at the artworks, relax in the gardens, and walk the nature trail.

Limestone quarried for the development of Coral Gables produced an irregularly shaped quarry pit. In 1924-25, the site was developed as the Venetian Pool, with a waterfall, sand beach, and landscaping. The attraction formerly had a casino and still has its Venetian bridge, towers, and lamp posts. Its visitors included Johnny Weissmuller.

Another Coral Gables attraction is the Biltmore Hotel and Country Club, built in 1925-26 with a 26-story replica of the Giralda Bell Tower of the Cathedral of Seville. Since 1926, when this photograph was taken, its guests have included Bing Crosby, Rudy Vallee, Judy Garland, Ginger Rogers, and Dwight Eisenhower, who came to swim, golf, and be seen.

On 30 acres south of Miami is a reserve inhabited by nearly 400 primates of 30 different species, including more than 80 Java monkeys descended from 6 released into the area in 1933 by Joseph DuMond. Visitors wander the grounds and watch monkeys finding and eating natural foods, and attend regularly scheduled feedings where the monkeys dive into a pool to retrieve fruit thrown in by park workers. Monkey Jungle has more than just monkeys. It now includes orangutans and their habitat. Also popular are the alligators, King the lowland gorilla, and the chimpanzee twins. This image dates from the 1940s.

The grounds and adjacent beach at the south end of Key Biscayne have long been a tourist destination, as shown in this photograph of the Cape Florida Lighthouse from 1926. Today visitors can also tour the tower and keeper's house.

In 1948, Miami's Crandon Park Zoo was established by the purchase of a goat, two black bears, and three monkeys at a cost of $270. They had been part of a small road show, which became stranded near Miami, and were moved to their new home on Key Biscayne.

In 1957, a group of Miami residents founded the Gold Coast Railroad Museum to preserve the history of a portion of Florida's railroads. Included in the collection are the two engines shown here. On the left is Florida East Coast Railway no. 153, which pulled the rescue train from Marathon after the 1935 hurricane. On the right is no. 113, constructed in 1913 and used by the FEC for regular service. Both were donated by the U.S. Sugar Corp. Another popular item is the *Ferdinand Magellan*, a private Pullman railroad car built for President Franklin Roosevelt, and also used by presidents Truman, Eisenhower, and Reagan. The museum is located on a former World War II blimp base in Miami.

In Key West there is a site which draws many tourists every year, even though there is little to do there other than take pictures. It is the Southernmost Point of the United States (at least, if Hawaii isn't counted), located at the end of Whitehurst Street. During the late 1930s, Jim Kee started selling sea shells at the site, not unlike the ones shown here in 1970. The site was marked with a wooden sign, which made a good backdrop for photos, but which was repeatedly stolen. To prevent further thefts, a buoy-shaped concrete marker took its place in 1983. The site is not actually Key West's southernmost point—one can continue south to the water, or even farther, on the naval base nearby.

The Ernest Hemingway Home and Museum was built in 1851 by merchant Asa Tift. Instead of the usual wood, he built it of native stone with a Spanish colonial style. From 1931 until his death in 1961, it was the home of author Ernest Hemingway. Visitors come to see his writing studio, safari souvenirs, and Key West's first swimming pool.

The Audubon House and Tropical Gardens of Key West became the island's first restoration project in 1958 when it was saved from demolition. The home had been built by the 1840s for sea captain John Geiger, and is surrounded by peaceful gardens. Inside are 28 works of art by naturalist John James Audubon, who visited the area in 1832.

The Key West City Cemetery was established in 1847 after a hurricane destroyed earlier ones. It sits on 19 acres in the middle of Key West and the number buried there has been estimated to be between 60,000 and 100,000. At first glance, the cemetery reminds one of those in New Orleans, where many tombs are built above ground level.

In Key West, families often stack remains three or fours tiers high, or the same beneath the ground, so that many relatives can be interred in a single small plot. One of the most visited sites within the cemetery is the USS *Maine* memorial, behind an iron picket fence, where a bronze sailor statue stands guard over the remains of 27 who died in the 1898 sinking in Havana.

In 1929, Richter Perky constructed a large bat tower to house bats, which according to plan would eat Sugarloaf Key's mosquitoes so that he could develop a resort. Over nearly eight decades, the Bat Tower has attracted no bats, and one story tells of Perky bringing a thousand bats from New Jersey, which immediately flew away. The 30-foot tower does attract tourists.

Built for defense during the Civil War, the West Martello Tower, Joe Allen Garden Center of Key West is one of the area's few free tourist attractions. In the mid-1950s, the ruin was made available to the Key West Garden Club, which renovated it and planted beautiful gardens, which attract locals and visitors. Very popular is the orchid arbor.

At Treasure Harbor on Plantation Key was the museum of Arthur McKee. He founded the Museum of Sunken Treasure to display the gold, cannon, idols, elephant tusks, and other artifacts he found as a deep-sea diver and treasure hunter, and some which he obtained from others. The attraction includes a glass-bottom boat from which visitors can watch divers working on a Spanish galleon wrecked nearby. A popular item is a pair of 75-pound bars of gold bullion. McKee found three of them in a Spanish wreck east of Key Largo, and the third one is on display in the Smithsonian. McKee opened the museum in a small building in 1949 and replaced it in 1952. The structure resembling a fortress has been converted into Treasure Village, a collection of art and gift shops.

Key West's Wrecker's Museum is located in the island's oldest house, built around 1829 and occupied by the family of Captain Francis B. Watlington from the 1830s until the 1930s. He was a professional wrecker, salvaging cargo from sunken ships. Its age and architecture alone attract tourists, and inside are displays depicting the wrecking industry.

A popular means of seeing the sites of Key West, which itself has become a tourist attraction, is the Conch Tour Train. More than 10 million visitors have ridden the wheeled vehicles, which claim to be the successors to Henry Flagler's railroad that connected the Keys to the mainland. The popular trains have run since 1958.

The world's second-oldest marine park is Theater of the Sea, located in Islamorada. As shown here in 1956, a leading attraction has always been the performing aquatic mammals. Today the visitor can swim with the dolphins, touch sharks, and be kissed by sea lions. The performing bottle-nosed dolphins can best be enjoyed in a natural coral grotto, visited as part of a two-hour tour, which includes views of rays and sharks. The park was opened in 1946 by the McKenney family, utilizing for its lagoon a former quarry that had provided stone for Henry M. Flagler's Overseas Highway, connecting Key West to the Florida mainland by railroad.

Key West was hit hard by the Great Depression and turned over its charter to the federal government. Federal officials decided that Key West could be a great tourist destination because of its geography and weather, and had the Works Progress Administration construct an open-air aquarium in 1932-34. The Key West Aquarium is still a popular tourist destination today, and is nearly twice the size of the original facility, with its outdoor holding pens and Atlantic Shores exhibit.

At the Key West Aquarium, shown here in a 1935 photograph, the animals could be viewed in a series of outdoor pools, easily reachable by visitors.

The five-sided Fort Clinch was constructed to protect the area near Fernandina Beach beginning in 1847. It was occupied by troops during the Civil and Spanish-American wars, then was abandoned. The state acquired it in 1935, and in 1938 it was opened to the public. Actors in nineteenth-century costumes and historical displays are popular with tourists.

By the mid-1960s, along US 98 east of Destin sat the Museum of the Sea and Indian, with displays of Indian artifacts and ocean life. An alligator and several small animals were displayed in a small pool and cages, and most of the diorama exhibits were housed in sheds without air conditioning. The attraction was destroyed by Hurricane Opal in 1995.

Tupperware, which produces plastic containers (some of which can be worn, as shown in this 1960 photo), moved from Massachusetts to Orlando in 1952. The large campus it opened south of downtown included the company's world headquarters, a large auditorium, and a surprisingly interesting display of food containers through the ages.

The small, unincorporated community of Christmas has sometimes been known as Fort Christmas because of its proximity to the site of an 1830s fort. December is always a busy time for the Christmas post office, with many people wanting a "Christmas" postmark on their holiday mail. On November 3, 1969, the community was selected for the First Day issuance of a Christmas stamp, at the time only the tenth Florida locale chosen as a First Day post office. One of the old post offices was converted into the Old Post Office Museum, featuring ornaments that have hung on National Christmas Trees outside the White House. Outside is a tall permanent Christmas tree decorated year-round.

Billed as "Orlando's Largest and Finest Motel," Wigwam Village built in 1948 consisted of 31 buildings resembling Plains Indians homes arranged in a horseshoe shape. Only the main wigwam was air conditioned, but the motel became a popular tourist destination. The motel rooms, gift shop, restaurant, and auto service station were razed in 1973.

Heartbreak Hotel was built in 1915 in Kenansville and was known as the Piney Woods Inn and the Tropical Hotel. In the 1940s, it was purchased by James W. Webb of Kentucky. When Elvis Presley's song "Heartbreak Hotel" became a hit in 1956, Webb renamed his inn, and reporters, photographers, and tourists flocked to it for decades. Webb allowed them to continue believing (erroneously) that it was the inspiration for Presley's song.

Shown here in 1957 is Bill Silvers, proprietor of the St. Cloud China and Clock Museum, taking two hours a week to wind 192 of the 317 clocks on display. For decades, the museum was a popular attraction for those who enjoyed clocks, figurines, lamps, sculpture, and a wide variety of knickknacks and treasures.

Ancient America was a project of Esmond G. Barnhill, who also operated an Indian trading post in the summer in Wisconsin and later founded Florida attractions known as the Indian Springs Museum and the Indian World Museum and Trading Post. At Ancient America in 1953, he tunneled out an ancient Calusa mound and installed glass walls so tourists could view its contents. He also displayed relics from shipwrecks and native artifacts dating back to the arrival of the Spanish, and had murals painted to depict early Indian culture. He gave up after a few years because few tourists visited his 25-acre attraction along US 1 in Boca Raton. The land was later developed as the community of Sanctuary.

James Melton hosted NBC's Ford Festival in the early 1950s, a TV show sponsored by the Ford Motor Company. Melton collected Fords and other cars beginning in 1936, and opened his James Melton Autorama in the early 1950s in Hypoluxo to display them to the public. In addition to almost 100 cars were baby carriages, toys, and music boxes. "America the Beautiful" was a large cyclorama on-site, treating visitors to images from American history. Melton died in 1961 and his museum closed soon afterward. According to the book *Bright Wheels Rolling,* the Autorama held America's most famous collection of automobiles—the author happened to be James Melton, whose susceptibility to bias one can only surmise.

An interesting archway at the Rainbow Tropical Gardens in 1941.

Florida's tourists have many choices when it comes to accommodations in which to stay while visiting theme parks and other attractions. Henry Flagler built hotels which became attractions unto themselves. The Royal Poinciana Hotel was built in 1894 and, along with the Breakers, another large luxury hotel nearby, provided winter accommodations for northern industrialists, financiers, and politicians, and European nobility. The Royal Poinciana was razed in 1936, but the Breakers—twice rebuilt—still attracts tourists.

Adjacent their gift shop located in what is now known as Indian Shores, Trader Frank and Jo Byars developed 4 acres into Tiki Gardens in 1962. By 1969, the gardens with a South Pacific theme had been expanded to 12 acres and included several gift shops, monkeys and birds, and Trader Frank's restaurant. They sold the attraction in 1986 to foreign investors, who initially intended to construct a hotel, but changed their minds and sold the property to the county in 1990 for $3 million. The huge tikis—on the page opposite—were sold and the buildings were razed to make way for a parking lot and access to Tiki Gardens Beach.

Although there had been tropical-themed parks in the state in prior years, they were joined by African-themed parks with the opening of Africa USA in Loxahatchee in 1954. Its popularity was surpassed by Lion Country Safari, which appeared in West Palm Beach in 1967. Lion Country, shown here, was begun by entrepreneurs from England and South Africa and was advertised as the first drive-through "cageless zoo," since visitors were allowed to drive through in their own vehicles. They could also ride the Everglades Express tour train shown on the following page. Tourists were the animals on display as much as were the lions, giraffes, zebras, and chimpanzees brought in from Africa, who would approach the cars to peer inside. It still attracts tourists who come to see the more than 900 animals in a natural setting.

In 1914, Robert S. Brown had a house built along the west side of Druid Road in Belleair and named his estate Century Oaks because of its large live oak trees. Brown made his fortune by patenting paint used on every Ford automobile in the early 1920s. The estate was purchased by Nigel Mansell, a famous formula-one race car driver. Fumio Hawakawa transformed much of the property into the Japanese Eaglenest Gardens in 1938, landscaping 65 acres. Because of anti-Japanese sentiment following World War II, it was renamed Eaglenest Gardens in 1945. It was a restful spot where residents and tourists could dine or enjoy afternoon tea from December to May. The land was later subdivided and sold for homesites.

Tussaud's London Wax Museum opened in St. Pete Beach in 1963, capitalizing on the family name of the famed museum in London. It was established by T. Alec Rigby, a partner in the Ripley's museum company. It featured more than 120 wax figures in scenes from movies, history, TV, and, of course, a chamber of horrors. Its manager, Ted Stambaugh, purchased the museum in 1978 and attempted to attract more tourists by adding recognizable figures from recent popular movies, but it was still a wax museum and audiences preferred the moving figures found in the larger theme parks. The museum closed on January 15, 1989, with plans for reopening in a new building, which never came to fruition.

Richard and June Baumgardner opened the Kapok Tree Restaurant in Clearwater adjacent a very large kapok tree in 1957, with family-style meals in several grand dining rooms and opulent outdoor gardens. The restaurant went out of business and the building was remodeled as retail space. The gardens are available for events such as proms and weddings.

In 1964, the Aquatarium was constructed by Marine Attractions on 17 acres on St. Pete Beach. It sat between 64th and 66th avenues and had a great view of the Gulf of Mexico. The main structures were a golden geodesic dome standing 160 feet tall and an outdoor amphitheater beside a large performance pool. Porpoises, pilot whales, and sea lions were among the animals featured at the park. By the 1980s, the Aquatarium was having financial troubles, so the owner petitioned for permission to add amusement-park rides to the animal-based attraction. The city turned down the request and the attraction closed for good.

When MGM Studios filmed a 1962 remake of the 1935 film *Mutiny on the Bounty,* it had a replica built of the sailing ship used in the original movie. After the remake starring Marlon Brando was released, the ship was turned into a tourist attraction in St. Petersburg. Called MGM's Bounty Exhibit, it included both the ship moored at the municipal pier, a replica of the longboat in which Captain Bligh and a few other sailors were sent from the ship following the real mutiny, and a replica of a Tahitian village. On the ship, visitors heard recorded scenes from the 1935 movie starring Charles Laughton and Clark Gable, not the actors for whom the replica was built. The ship is still in St. Petersburg for part of the year, and can also be seen in *Pirates of the Caribbean: Dead Man's Chest.*

George Turner in 1903 purchased six acres in St. Petersburg. He drained a lake and planted the rich muck soil with bananas, vegetables, and flowers. He then fenced in the property, named it Sunken Gardens, and by the 1920s began charging a nickel for tours. During the late 1940s, son Ralph Turner brought in exotic animals such as monkeys, flamingos, and parrots. He also added wax figures depicting the life of Christ. By the 1970s, attendance had fallen off and the formerly elaborate attraction was downsized. Sunken Gardens was purchased by the city in 1999 and is operated as a botanical park featuring special presentations on caring for plants.

Owner Earl L. Smith made it a point to personally greet visitors to his USA of Yesterday Museum along US 27 in Dundee. It opened about the same time as Walt Disney World, and Smith hoped that he would meet lots of tourists with an interest in early American mechanical innovations, such as this 1931 Packard roadster. Unfortunately for him, most tourists either remained in the Magic Kingdom or rushed by to get to Cypress Gardens. The property was soon redeveloped for industry.

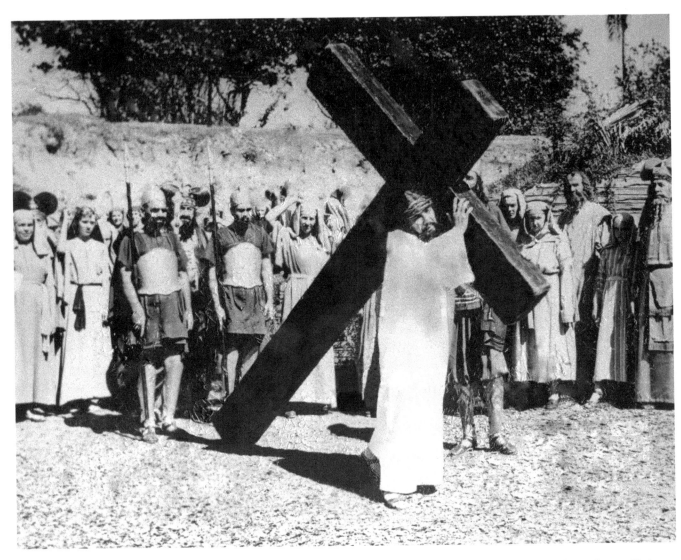

In 1932, Josef Meier of Germany formed a touring theatrical company to perform a reenactment of the last days of Jesus Christ. Meier starred in the Christ role and in 1939 established a permanent home for his production in Spearfish in the Black Hills of South Dakota. A Lake Wales amphitheater was constructed as its winter home and the Black Hills Passion Play opened there in 1953. Shown here is a 1953 scene from the popular play, which ran until 1998. The empty amphitheater in 2002 became the home of the Life of Christ Passion Play, brought to Lake Wales from Tennessee by Jimmy Baker, who portrayed the title character.

Frank Lloyd Wright came to Florida Southern College in Lakeland in 1938 to exploit his designs in an educational setting. He worked for nearly 20 years to develop his Child of the Sun collection of 18 campus buildings. Although several were eliminated before they left the drawing board, those which were constructed are very different from buildings found on other college campuses and continue to attract tourists. Much of the work was performed by students, who earned a portion of their tuition fees by manufacturing concrete blocks and pouring concrete floors and walkways. Shown here in 1947 is the E. T. Roux Library designed by Wright and his protégés.

Since the early days, Spook Hill has attracted those who've heard that if one places his car in neutral and releases the brake, it will roll uphill. Signs along the road in Lake Wales give instructions on where to park and what to expect.

The landscape creates an optical illusion that makes it look like the vehicle is going uphill.

Considered by many to be Florida's first real theme park, Cypress Gardens was the creation of Richard Downing "Dick" Pope, Sr., during the 1930s. He turned lake and marsh near Winter Haven into a tourist mecca, which still exists today. Opening January 2, 1936, the attraction was a showplace for flowers from around the world, and soon added the Southern Belles, a crew of attractive women in hoopskirts to serve as focal points for the color. Water ski shows and boat rides along the canals soon became popular. Esther Williams movies were filmed here, as were television shows. The Rotating Island in the Sky ride was added in 1983, followed soon by an ice-skating show. The attraction closed for a while but is again popular with tourists.

A water-ski show is in progress at Cypress Gardens.

The ornamental Ravine State Gardens were created by the WPA in 1933 and were maintained by the city of Palatka until 1970. They became part of the Florida State Park System that year. Water flowing under a sandy ridge flanking the western shore of the St. Johns River created the steep ravine in the gardens. Grasses and shrubs gradually covered the slopes of the ravine, slowing down the process of erosion. Eventually, trees also became established and formed the present mixed hardwood forest. Since the park's opening, it has attracted visitors who wish to hike, picnic, or just view the atypical Florida landscape.

In 1964, a 2,000-seat outdoor amphitheater was constructed near St. Augustine for the performance of *Cross and Sword*, a new state play written by Paul Green. The production was expensive to stage, with music, dance, and drama, and as the amphitheater aged it required more and more maintenance. Initially, *Cross and Sword* was automatically funded by the state, but later had to compete with other state-supported arts. It also experienced a decline in attendance as other tourist attractions rose in popularity. Its 1997 request for state funding was denied, making 1996 its last season of production.

In 1946, James Casper opened an attraction called Casper's Ostrich and Alligator Farm, located about three miles north of downtown St. Augustine on US 1. There, he raised ostriches, rare birds, alligators, crocodiles, and other reptiles. Casper made money charging admission to see the live animals, raced the ostriches, and had a business importing hides from other countries. The St. Augustine attraction closed in 1982. Shown on the page opposite in 1948 are James Casper and the entrance to his attraction.

At 4 Artillery Lane in St. Augustine is a building that was used in the 1910s as a warehouse and garage. From the 1880s forward the building had housed the store of C. F. Hamblen, which by 1908 was Florida's third-largest hardware store. Hamblen's moved to King Street and the building was eventually transformed into the Oldest Store Museum shown here. It has now been converted to residences.

In 1938, a park opened south of St. Augustine called Marine Studios. It was the world's first underwater movie studio and marine mammal park for exhibition of dolphins and similar creatures in a more-or-less natural habitat. In the 1940s, the park was renamed Marineland to sound more like something tourists would want to visit, and for a time was the state's most successful tourist attraction. It still draws crowds, the favored attraction being the world's first trained-porpoise show, which opened in 1951.

Shown here in 1968 are tourists passing the Museum of Yesterday's Toys, which operated at 52 St. George Street in the Ancient City area of St. Augustine. The building dates to 1760, when it was the residence of Spanish army sergeant Fernando Rodriguez. After serving as a grocery store, it was restored in 1958 and is now a gift shop.

The Alcazar Hotel was constructed in 1888 to be a Henry Flagler destination, this one intended to serve a less affluent clientele than that of the Ponce de Leon. A dining room was added later and some of the shops were converted to a hotel lobby. The hotel closed in 1931. St. Augustine's City Hall and the Lightner Museum occupy the building today.

The popular Fountain of Youth attraction located on the site of an Indian burial ground, developed and promoted by Dr. Luella Day McConnell and later by entrepreneur Walter B. Fraser, allegedly includes a cross of stones placed in the ground by Juan Ponce de Leon in 1513. On display is a spring, around which a well was built in 1875, located within a cypress and coquina spring house. The St. Augustine attraction also includes a pewter reproduction of a salt cellar, an area believed to be the Indian village of Seloy, and other exhibits relating to Indian and Spanish occupation of the area.

In the early 1890s, Felix Fire and George Reddington began exhibiting about 40 penned-up alligators at the beach at the end of a tram railway that crossed Anastasia Island, calling it the South Beach Alligator Farm and Museum of Marine Curiosities. The facility was bought in 1937 by W. I. Drysdale and F. Charles Usina, who combined it with Joseph Campbell's Jacksonville alligator farm, calling it the St. Augustine Alligator Farm. It was badly damaged by a fire, but they rebuilt and expanded it. Popular among military personnel stationed in Florida during World War II, by their telling others about it, it became a leading tourist destination and still draws crowds today.

Shown in this photo from 1966 is the dolphin show at Osprey's Floridaland, which also included a western town with shoot-outs, a saloon show, and a tour train (a trackless wheeled tram). In its attempt to pick elements from other Florida attractions, it also had an entrance with colorful birds and a petting zoo. Floridaland, which advertised "Everything Under the Sun," opened in December 1964 and closed in the early 1970s.

Children study the flamingos fishing in a lagoon at Sarasota Jungle Gardens.

121

From 1955 until 1959, on Proctor Road just east of Sarasota was the attraction known as Sunshine Springs and Gardens. Twenty acres of landscaped tropical gardens were viewed from swan boats traveling along a series of canals. On a 400-acre artificial lake were held water-ski shows featuring female "aquabelles" and a trained elephant.

Opening in 1953 under the name of Horn's Cars of Yesterday, and then attracting tourists under the name of Bellm's Cars and Music of Yesterday starting in the 1960s, the Sarasota Classic Car Museum is one of the world's oldest car museums. In addition to more than a hundred cars, there are also displays of antique cameras, games, and photos.

The John and Mable Ringling Museum of Art was established in 1927 on the Ringlings' 66-acre Sarasota estate. The museum features 21 galleries of American and European paintings, antiquities from Cyprus, Asian art, and modern works. The most famous piece in the collection is a cast of Michelangelo's *David*, shown here, which overlooks a beautifully landscaped courtyard.

The Ringling Museum of the American Circus in Sarasota opened in 1948 to document and display circus history. On display are antique posters, handbills, business records, costumes, props, equipment, and elaborate circus wagons such as the one pictured here in 1954. On display in the learning center is the world's largest miniature replica circus.

Warm Mineral Springs near the Myakka River is known for its free-flowing artesian spring, which fills a sinkhole with healthy mineral water at a temperature of 87 degrees. In 1953, an underwater explorer diving in the springs discovered stalactites and stalagmites below the water's surface, indicating that the site was for a very long time a dry cave.

Sarasota's Circus Hall of Fame, pictured here in 1966 in its leased buildings, was attracting 80,000 visitors a year until 1979, when the land which it leased was sold and the attraction was forced to close or move. The collection was acquired by a group from Peru, Indiana, at a cost of $450,000. They relocated the facility to their town and expanded its scope and size.

The Asolo State Theater was built in Asolo, Italy, in 1798 by Antonio Locatelli. It was dismantled during the 1930s and stored by Adolph Loewi of Venice. In 1937, it was seen by Chick Austin and, when he became Director of the Ringling Museum of Art in 1946, he arranged for its purchase. The Asolo Theater opened in Sarasota in 1952.

The Central Florida Zoo started out as the Sanford Zoo in 1923 when the Sanford Fire Department was given a collection of animals. They were moved in 1941 to a site where the present City Hall sits. The expanding zoo was later moved again to a site west of downtown and reopened on July 4, 1975, with its present name and much more natural habitats.

Rainforest opened along US 301 north of Bushnell in the 1960s. Tourists who stopped found a welcome center, trails with animated animal models, and real animals such as ostriches. Its Sacred Art Garden displayed unusual painted works. By the end of the decade, attendance dropped and all that remained was the life-size roadside dinosaur and boarded-up building.

During the 1950s and early 1960s, the area known as Salem along US 98 had a tourist stop known as Florida Reptile Land. A free zoo claiming to hold more than a hundred kinds of animals from all over the world enticed people to have a look. The attraction made its money from the sale of gasoline, pecans, jellies, coffee, hot dogs, candy, and souvenirs.

The attraction known as the Sugar Mill Gardens began to attract tourists under the name of Bongoland in 1948, when Manny Lawrence opened the park to the public. Featured were life-size concrete dinosaur sculptures, a train ride, and a baboon named Bongo. The Port Orange park closed in 1952 and in 1963 it was donated to the county.

The dinosaurs and paths of Bongoland are still around, but the main draw today is the ruins of an old sugar mill and outbuildings constructed on the plantation of Patrick Dean, who acquired the land in 1804. Named Dun-Lawton in the 1830s, the farm was partly destroyed during the Second Seminole War. Rebuilt, it continued as a working plantation into the mid-1850s.

With a depth of 185 feet, Wakulla Springs is known as the world's deepest spring. It produces more than 600,000 gallons of water each minute. Tourists began arriving soon after the Civil War and moviemakers started filming during the mid-1940s. The Wakulla Springs Lodge, constructed during 1937 by financier Edward Ball, still offers fine Southern food in its dining room. The 2,888 acres can be viewed on foot, in glass-bottom boats, or as part of a jungle cruise. Divers in the spring have found a diverse collection of items, including fossilized mastodon bones, one of which is being examined by the diver in this image. Visitors were allowed on the property when it was privately owned. The state purchased the area in 1986 and made it a state park.

# Notes on the Photographs

These notes, listed by page number, attempt to include all aspects known of the photographs. Each of the photographs is identified by the page number, a title or description, photographer and collection, archive, and call or box number when applicable. Although every attempt was made to collect all data, in some cases complete data may have been unavailable due to the age and condition of some of the photographs and records.

34 **SULPHUR SPRINGS**
Florida State
Archives
Rc10961

35 **BALLAST POINT
PARK**
Florida State
Archives
Rc13556

36 **RATTLESNAKE**
Florida State
Archives
PR02440

37 **PALMA CEIA
SPRING**
Florida State
Archives
N042057

38 **LOWRY PARK**
Florida State
Archives
Pc5719

39 **MCKEE JUNGLE
GARDENS**
Florida State
Archives
N048396

40 **TWO EGG**
Florida State
Archives
FP831887

41 **FLORIDA CAVERNS
STATE PARK**
Florida State
Archives
PR10740

42 **VENETIAN GARDENS**
Florida State
Archives
N048146

43 **EVERGLADES
WONDER GARDEN**
Florida State
Archives
C013564

44 **ALFRED B.
MACLAY GARDENS
STATE PARK**
Florida State
Archives
C029790

45 **TALLAHASSEE
MUSEUM OF
HISTORY AND
NATURAL SCIENCE**
Florida State
Archives
C038468

46 **MANATEE SPRINGS
STATE PARK**
Florida State
Archives
C027341

47 **GREGORY HOME,
TORREYA STATE
PARK**
Florida State
Archives
Rc09539

48 **GARDEN OF EDEN**
Florida State
Archives
RK0530

49 **SILVER SPRINGS**
Florida State
Archives
PR15191

50 **SIX GUN
TERRITORY**
Florida State
Archives
C630460

51 **CARRIAGE
CAVALCADE**
Florida State
Archives
N041747

52 **ROSS ALLEN'S
REPTILE INSTITUTE**
Florida State
Archives
N041747

53 **EARLY AMERICAN
MUSEUM**
Florida State
Archives
C630445

54 **RAINBOW SPRINGS**
Florida State
Archives
C024930

55 **RAINBOW SPRINGS
NO. 2**
Florida State
Archives
C014786

56 **ELLIOTT MUSEUM**
Florida State
Archives
PC4146

57 **HOUSE OF REFUGE
MUSEUM AT
GILBERT'S BAR**
Florida State
Archives
Rc08715

58 **CORAL CASTLE**
Florida State
Archives
C621897

59 **MIAMI SEAQUARIUM**
Florida State
Archives
C022099

60 **DOLPHINS AT
SEAQUARIUM**
Florida State
Archives
C022100

61 **MUSA ISLE INDIAN
VILLAGE**
Florida State
Archives
PR04785

62 **FAIRCHILD
TROPICAL BOTANIC
GARDEN**
Florida State
Archives
C024244

63 **MIAMI
SERPENTARIUM**
Florida State
Archives
C019636

64 **MIAMI BEACH
AQUARIUM**
Florida State
Archives
Rc15129

65 **VIZCAYA**
Florida State
Archives
Rc19091

66 **THE VENETIAN
POOL**
Florida State
Archives
Rc00-126

67 **BILTMORE HOTEL
AND COUNTRY
CLUB**
Florida State
Archives
Rc11798

68 **MONKEY JUNGLE**
Florida State
Archives
C003652

69 **CAPE FLORIDA
LIGHTHOUSE**
Florida State
Archives
Rc03156

70 **CRANDON PARK
ZOO**
Florida State
Archives
N031725

71 **GOLD COAST
RAILROAD MUSEUM**
Florida State
Archives
Rc13515

72 **SOUTHERNMOST
POINT**
Florida State
Archives
C676249

73 **ERNEST
HEMINGWAY HOME**
Florida State
Archives
Rc07404

74 **AUDUBON HOUSE
AND TROPICAL
GARDENS**
Florida State
Archives
C039528

75 **KEY WEST CITY
CEMETERY**
Florida State
Archives
C007338

76 **USS MAINE
MEMORIAL AT
KEY WEST CITY
CEMETERY**
Florida State
Archives
C025994

77 **BAT TOWER**
Florida State
Archives
RC18093

78 **WEST MARTELLO
TOWER**
Florida State
Archives
C679791

79 **MUSEUM OF
SUNKEN TREASURE**
Florida State
Archives
AM0170

80 WRECKER'S MUSEUM
Florida State
Archives
DM1404

81 CONCH TOUR TRAIN
Florida State
Archives
C620354

82 THEATER OF THE SEA
Florida State
Archives
C684605

83 KEY WEST AQUARIUM
Florida State
Archives
C032324

84 KEY WEST AQUARIUM INTERIOR
Florida State
Archives
N033433

85 FORT CLINCH
Florida State
Archives
C019353

86 MUSEUM OF THE SEA AND INDIAN
Florida State
Archives
C670858

87 TUPPERWARE
Florida State
Archives
C033886

88 FORT CHRISTMAS
Florida State
Archives
C008521

89 WIGWAM VILLAGE
Florida State
Archives
C022488

90 HEARTBREAK HOTEL
Florida State
Archives
N033369

91 ST. CLOUD CHINA AND CLOCK MUSEUM
Florida State
Archives
C025094

92 ANCIENT AMERICA
Florida State
Archives
AM0144

93 JAMES MELTON AUTORAMA
Florida State
Archives
C018567

94 RAINBOW TROPICAL GARDENS
Florida State
Archives
PHA224A

95 ROYAL POINCIANA HOTEL
Florida State
Archives
N036611

96 TIKI GARDENS
Florida State
Archives
C651462

97 LION COUNTRY SAFARI
Florida State
Archives
C677464

98 LION COUNTRY SAFARI NO. 2
Florida State
Archives
C681846

99 JAPANESE EAGLENEST GARDENS
Florida State
Archives
PHA049

100 TUSSAUD'S LONDON WAX MUSEUM
Florida State
Archives
C621596

101 KAPOK TREE RESTAURANT
Florida State
Archives
C684933

102 AQUATARIUM
Florida State
Archives
C640244

103 MGM's BOUNTY EXHIBIT
Florida State
Archives
C673372

104 SUNKEN GARDENS
Florida State
Archives
C630346

105 USA OF YESTERDAY
Florida State
Archives
PC0923

106 LIFE OF CHRIST PASSION PLAY
Florida State
Archives
RC18196

107 FLORIDA SOUTHERN COLLEGE
Florida State
Archives
C008441

108 SPOOK HILL
Florida State
Archives
RC12642

109 CYPRESS GARDENS
Florida State
Archives
N041400

110 CYPRESS GARDENS WATER-SKI SHOW
Florida State
Archives
C0621968

111 RAVINE STATE GARDENS
Florida State
Archives
RC20322

112 CROSS AND SWORD
Florida State
Archives
PR13801

113 CASPER'S OSTRICH AND ALLIGATOR FARM
Florida State
Archives
C002764

114 OLDEST STORE MUSEUM
Florida State
Archives
C800513

115 MARINELAND
Florida State
Archives
C039056

116 MUSEUM OF YESTERDAY'S TOYS
Florida State
Archives
C672716

117 ALCAZAR HOTEL
Florida State
Archives
Rc06993

118 TO THE FOUNTAIN OF YOUTH
Florida State
Archives
Pr09538

119 ST. AUGUSTINE ALLIGATOR FARM
Florida State
Archives
PR00132

120 FLORIDALAND
Florida State
Archives
C660614

121 SARASOTA JUNGLE GARDENS
Florida State
Archives
Rc27051

122 SUNSHINE SPRINGS AND GARDENS
Florida State
Archives
c023042

123 SARASOTA CLASSIC CAR MUSEUM
Florida State
Archives
C660572

124 JOHN AND MABLE RINGLING MUSEUM OF ART
Florida State
Archives
Pr09438

125 RINGLING MUSEUM OF THE AMERICAN CIRCUS
Florida State
Archives
C019707

126 WARM MINERAL SPRINGS
Florida State
Archives
C031798

# BIBLIOGRAPHY

Brown, Robert H. "Florida's Lost Tourist Attractions." www.lostparks.com.

Carlson, Charlie. *Weird Florida.* New York: Barnes & Noble Books, 2005.

Gleasner, Diana and Bill. *Florida Off the Beaten Path: A Guide to Unique Places.* Guilford, Conn.: Globe Pequot Press, 2003.

Hollis, Tim. *Dixie Before Disney: 100 Years of Roadside Fun.* Jackson: University Press of Mississippi, 1999.

———. *Florida's Miracle Strip: From Redneck Riviera to Emerald Coast.* Jackson: University Press of Mississippi, 2004.

Kleinberg, Eliot. *Historical Traveler's Guide to Florida.* Sarasota, Fla.: Pineapple Press, 1997.

Monaghan, Kelly. *Orlando's Other Theme Parks: What To Do When You've Done Disney.* New York: Intrepid Traveler, 1999.

Waitley, Douglas. *Roadside History of Florida.* Missoula, Mont.: Mountain Press Publishing Company, 1997.

Printed in the USA
CPSIA information can be obtained
at www.ICGtesting.com
JSHW072021140824
68134JS00042B/3730

9 781683 368298